YOUR KNOWLEDGE HAS VALUE

- We will publish your bachelor's and
  master's thesis, essays and papers

- Your own eBook and book -
  sold worldwide in all relevant shops

- Earn money with each sale

Upload your text at www.GRIN.com
and publish for free

Bibliographic information published by the German National Library:

The German National Library lists this publication in the National Bibliography; detailed bibliographic data are available on the Internet at http://dnb.dnb.de .

Imprint:

Copyright © 2019 GRIN Verlag
Print and binding: Books on Demand GmbH, Norderstedt Germany
ISBN: 9783668976962

This book at GRIN:

https://www.grin.com/document/480695

Mustapha Abdullah Kuyateh

Values in Society and Religion

GRIN Verlag

GRIN - Your knowledge has value

Since its foundation in 1998, GRIN has specialized in publishing academic texts by students, college teachers and other academics as e-book and printed book. The website www.grin.com is an ideal platform for presenting term papers, final papers, scientific essays, dissertations and specialist books.

Visit us on the internet:

http://www.grin.com/

http://www.facebook.com/grincom

http://www.twitter.com/grin_com

RELIGION AND HUMAN VALUES

IUCG

LEVEL 400
M.A. KUYATEH

TABLE OF CONTENTS

INTRODUCTION

By helping social norms to be internalized, values are indirectly sources of relationship behaviour. Likewise, cultural traditions, religion and language have different meanings that shape beliefs and influence social life. Thus, it seems important to reevaluate the role of values in social life in a society which is extremely distinguishable in religious terms. This course will therefore aid students in understanding the basic human values in selected religions around the globe. It will project some acceptable and non-acceptable values within society; and will guide us as to the role of religion in each of these values. Human values are social and ethical norms common to all cultures and societies as well as religions. They represent a melding of social progress, justice and spiritual growth. Practices are also time-bound, dictating how you should dress, what name you are to take, what you can eat, how many wives you may have, how a person should be punished if they make some mistake. In all traditions you find practices like these that were necessary at the time they were instituted, but they may no longer serve a good purpose today. In the Qur'an, it is prescribed that if someone steals, their hand must be cut off. At one time a Christian who wanted to be religious had to take a vow of poverty. Jains were not allowed to touch money (this dilemma was solved by having someone accompany them to carry their money for them). Jews could do no work on the Sabbath. Those who follow this rule today cannot turn on a light switch.

COURSE OBJECTIVES:

Upon successful completion of this course, the student will be able to:

> Understand some basic human values, which include but not limited to a deep caring for all life, a responsible attitude toward the planet, nonviolence, compassion and love, friendliness and compassion, generosity and sharing, integrity, honesty and sincerity, moderation in one's activity, service, commitment and responsibility, peace, contentment, and enthusiasm. How religion contributes to each and every one of these values, will be of utmost importance to our study.

DETAILED OUTLINE:

- **Sources of values.**
  This shall include some basic human values such as Self-Direction, Stimulation, Hedonism, Achievement, Power, Security, Conformity, Tradition, Benevolence, and Universalism. Additionally, theory, methods, and applications of these Values will be of immense importance to this course.
- **Human values.**
  This introduction presents the case of universal values and that of values and social change. This also includes moral values which shall be looked at from both the scientific

approach, and on the basis of ideologies. Discussion on secular values which include both global and local values shall be dealt with.

- **Religious values.**
A striking characteristic of contemporary philosophy is the attention given to theory of value. The subject has been given a new and more empirical turn by the work of Meinong and his followers. It is hoped that various ways will be suggested in applying the results of such an empirical analysis and classification of values to the study of religion.

- **Religious values and public policy.**
The area of discussion for this topic is the role of religion-based values and religious leaders in public policy debates. Consider what we hear about religion from some prominent persons in Ghana. Some question the legitimacy of religious-based values in public policy debates. Some also question the appropriateness of churches or religious leaders taking any public position on political issues.

- **Religious and human values in war and peace.**
World religions make use of the scripture to justify their actions, which are ultimately deployed in the context of war and peace. It is arguably evident that scriptural passages have been quoted as the guiding principles for the engagement in warfare and the establishment of peace. However, the question of the innocent lives that get perish in such cases, the lost of properties, as well as the issue of human dignity is paramount for our discussion. How do we maintain a peaceful coexistence based on universal human value system, shall all be the focus of this topic. This implies that scriptural knowledge is vital when analyzing the religious values on war and peace, especially in societies whereby religion is used as a motivation and justification of war and peace.

- **The universal role of religion in social life.**
Key issues to note here is that Religious practice appears to have enormous potential for addressing today's social problems. Also, Strong and repeated evidence indicates that the regular practice of religion has beneficial effects in nearly every aspect of social concern, which needs to be looked at critically by students. Again, Legislators should seek constitutionally appropriate ways to explore the impact of religious practice on society and, where appropriate, recognize its role especially in Ghana.

- **Religion, human values and politics.**
Student will learn from this topic that in a pluralist society such as Ghana, all values—including religious values—should be allowed on the political table and up for discussion. The inclusion of religious values within political debate is not only consistent with pluralist tenets but allows for moral discussion.

HUMAN VALUES

Human values are the virtues that guide us to take into account human element when one interacts with other human beings. They are our feelings for the human essence of others. It is both what we expect others to do to us and what we aim to give to other human beings. These human values give the effect of bonding, comforting and reassuring. Human values are universal and are important considerations to take into account, when interacting with other people. These values help to create bonding between people of different nationalities, race, religious beliefs and cultures.

Some basic values are -

i.	Self -direction
ii.	Stimulation
iii.	Hedonism
iv.	Achievement
v.	Power
vi.	Security
vii.	Conformity
viii.	Tradition
ix.	Benevolence
x.	Universalism

Other human values include, but not limited to love, kindness, justice, peace, honesty, respect, openness, loyalty and equality.

Today, human values play a great role in establishing peace and protecting society. Respect is one of the most essential values that people need to have. To show respect to a person, one must be able to appreciate that person's views, qualities and behaviors. A person should be willing to do to others what one expects other people to do to him or her. Ideally, respect is considered the most basic value from which all other social standards are derived.

Valuing the connection between human beings is important in creating peaceful coexistence and happiness. A person should be able to manage his or her reactions and feelings that could lead to misunderstandings or injury. Social standards help people to behave accordingly even when in a state of anger and to avoid any behavior lacking in respect.

Putting human values into practice helps to contribute towards morality within the society. By integrating human values with personal relations, a person can live in harmony with others.

Values can be independent variables, those at the origin of interests, habits, identity processes and social solidarity, but they can also be dependent variables, those deriving from other social factors. In both cases values have a central position. On a general consideration we might call them human values because they are linked with human subjects and their fundamental tendencies, and with their fundamental beliefs and evaluations, oriented to assume decisions.

The variety of human values is very wide. It is almost all-pervading. It embraces many fields: from knowledge to communication, from law to ethics and moral, from policy to economics, from education to medical and sanitary, from religion to secular, from daily life to general living.

A recurrent distinction concerns the difference between applied values and final values (Rokeac 1973)[1], therefore between values concerning individual practices and values which represent real goals to achieve.

---

[1] Inglehart R. (1977). *The Silent Revolution*, Princeton: Princeton University Press [This is a first contribution to the study of values in the European Community in the 1970 (6 countries) and in 1973 (9 countries)].

Another distinction quite widespread is between universal values and particular values. But the discussion is still open on which are the universal values. In particular the discussion tends to slip onto a juxtaposition of universal values and universal rights, which is to say between human values and human rights.

During the last Century the development of human rights has kept pace with the "scientification" process. An important increase of social and practical relevance of scientific and academic studies. Especially by the end of World War II, authority and influence of scientific research have been taken more into consideration, particularly in medical, economical and management fields (Drori, Meyer, Ramirez, Schofer 2003).[2] However, democratization dynamics, although growing, have not reached the level of human rights at the top of the scale. They passed from an interest with a few nations and organizations at the beginning of the 20th Century, to a number of more than three hundred organizations and nations directly involved by the end of the same Century. In this regard, the role of the so called high education has been decisive (Schofer, Meyer 2005).[3]

We can say that human rights widespread have become a world event. Therefore, it represents a significant modality in the more recent globalization processes. Problems of equality and exclusion, for instance, are a constant issue at the present time. They are a must in the international socio-political agenda. By now, the lack of participation of some groups – especially minorities, rural and of a low socialeconomical *status* – to higher education levels represents a strong call for attention and sensitivity for governments and international organizations.

Due to the Universal Declaration of Human Rights published by the United Nations, a strong interest for equality among individuals and for democratic participation values has been increasing for years. We shall now ask: "Are there other universal human rights?"

---

[2] Drori G., Meyer J. W., Ramirez F. O., Schofer E. (2003). *Science in the Modern World Polity: Institutionalization and Globalization*, Stanford (Cal.): Stanford University Press [This provides a general perspective on science and polity in a globalised world].
[3] Schofer E., Meyer J.W. (2005). *The Worldwide Expansion of Higher Education in the Twentieth Century*, American Sociological Review, December, 70, 6, 898-920 [This study is a report on the diffusion of higher education during last century].

As a matter of fact, what makes universal a human right is not a commonly shared opinion among nations. At most the Declaration can represent a valid reference, even if it has not been signed and fostered by all nations worldwide.

In absence of a commonly shared opinion among sociologists about the existence of values, sociological research can only give empirical surveys about the presence of average widespread values in each culture or socio-geographical and political context. Only a worldwide survey, using an appropriate and significant methodology, based on a comparative interpretation could provide general indications about the existence of meta-values, that is to say, values empirically found in various society that, when compared on a larger scale, may be indicated as universal.

In other words, values such as freedom, democracy, respect for individuals, "sacredness" of life, equality among individuals and others are not necessarily to be considered universal, just because they are prevailing in a certain part of the world. There are situations and conditions of various natures in the world which do not recognize such values, thus clearly showing that only a certain part of the world sustains and claims them as universal.

HUMAN VALUES THEORY AND AXIOLOGY

Throughout the 20th century psychologists and philosophers alike questioned whether human values could be studied in any meaningful way (Adler[4] 1956, Thurstone[5] 1959, Wickert[6] 1940) In the mid-twentieth century A.J. Ayers had argued that nothing meaningful could be said about human values and that someone making a value judgement was simply expressing some feelings (Ayers 1952)[7]. However, by the late twentieth century axiologists and philosophers had begun to reframe this problem. Frondizi noted that values had the quality of a gestalt (Gestaltqualität). Values could only be understood as a configuration of relative priorities. What was therefore needed was a theoretical model which treated values as organised into various patterns and configurations, rather than in discrete, uniquely measurable elements.

In the middle of the 20th century anthropologists were also making progress in their understanding of cultural values (Kroeber[8] 1952, Kroeber[9] and Kluckhohn 1963). They described human values as a conception, implicit or explicit, of the desirable which influenced the selection from available modes, means and ends of actions. Meanwhile, during the latter half of the 20th century, psychologists began to link human values with belief, attitude and emergent behaviour. Values were seen as conceptions of global beliefs related to end states or modes of behaviour underpinned by attitudinal processes and which could be linked to organisational

---

[4] Adler, F. (1956). The Value Concept in Sociology. American Journal of Sociology, 62:7.

[5] Thurstone, L. L. (1959). The Measurement of Values. Chicago: The University of Chicago Press.

[6] Wickert, F. (1940). A Test for Personal Goal Values. Journal of Social Psychology, 11:15.

[7] Ayers, A. J. (1952). Language, Truth & Logic.New York: Dover Publications.

[8] Kroeber, A. L. (1952). The Nature of Culture. Chicago University of Chicago Press.

[9] Kroeber, A. L., and C. Kluckhohn. (1963). Culture: A Critical Review of Concepts and Definitions. In Papers of the Peabody Museum of American Archaeology and Ethnology, edited by Alfred A. Knopf. New York: Vintage Edition.

outcomes (England and Lee[10] 1974, Rokeach[11] 1973). Schwartz and Bilsky used these ideas as a basis for a universal theory by viewing human values as cognitive and cultural representations of three general requirements particular to hominids (Schwartz and Bilsky 1987)[12]:

a. Biologically oriented needs of human individuals.
b. Social interaction needs which enable interpersonal coordination in community settings.
c. Institutional demands for community welfare and survival.

Human values transcended specific situations, guiding the selection or evaluation of behaviour and events in individual and collective contexts (Schwartz 2006)[13]. Values were prioritised relative to one another. It was this prioritisation which acted as the conceptual linchpin around which a perspective of value configurations could be constructed i.e. a theory in which human values were prioritised against one another in unique configurations associated with individuals as well as the communities in which they found themselves. This aligned well with anthropological perspectives of values, whilst also drawing on the important contribution of psychologists. Others had tried to develop similar models, the most notable being Hofstede. He had formulated a model which attempted to account for cultural differences between institutions and nations. It was based upon the idea of "mental programs" ((Hofstede 2001) p. xix)[14] which developed during early childhood and which were subsequently reinforced during education and by the institutions in which people worked as adults.

---

[10] England, G. W., and R. Lee. (1974). The Relationships between Managerial Values, Success in USA, Japan, India and Australia.Journal of Applied Psychology,59:8.

[11] Rokeach, M. (1973). The Nature of Human Values. New York: Free Press.

[12] Schwartz, S. H., and W. Bilsky. (1987). Toward A Psychological Structure of Human Values.Journal of Personality and Social Psychology, 53:12.

[13] Schwartz, S. (2006). Basic Human Values: Theory, Measurement and Applications. Revue Francaise de Sociologie,47 (4).

[14] Hofstede, G. (2001). Culture's Consequences: Comparing Values, Behaviours, Institutions, and Organisations Across Nations. 2nd ed. Thousand Oaks: Sage

The proposed model developed by Schwartz and his team was refined and by the mid-2000s a robust universal values model drawn from data gathered during a "World Values Survey" emerged which reflected the gestalt quality proposed by Frondizi. Hofstede's model had primarily been based on attitude survey data collected in the late-1960 and early 1970s from over a hundred thousand employees of IBM Corporation. The new model developed on the basis of the World Values Survey was drawn from similar samples sizes but gathered from the general populations of dozens and dozens of countries and not restricted to a single multinational organisation. Meaningful statements could now be made about both cultural and personal values. Evidence for a universal values model had now been found which seemed to hold up across cultural domains and which satisfied the requirements of Frondizi's axiology.

ON THE EUTHYPHRO DILEMMA: A RELIGIOUS FOUNDATION FOR ETHICS AND HUMAN VALUES?

Moral requirements like the duty not to kill or the duty to keep promises and so on, can naturally be thought of as commands. Following one's conscience can even feel as though one is following an "inner voice" of some kind. Could it be that moral duties are themselves reflections of the will of a good God, so that the moral requirement "Do not kill the innocent" is the equivalent or stems from "God prohibits the killing of the innocent"? Some philosophers have argued that the most reasonable account of the realm of morality is that it is constituted by divine commands and prohibitions. On this view, moral duties receive their binding character due to the agency of the Creator and, in the absence of God, morality would lose its objective authority. This stance has been developed in strong and moderate forms of a divine command theory of ethics and in the context of Platonic theism.

According to what might be called *the strong divine command theory*, there is an essential identity of morality and divine commands. So, what it means for someone to claim that killing the innocent is wrong is that God prohibits this. We have here a strict identity just as one has in the case of an analytic definition or in an identity relationship in the natural world. So, in terms of definitions, a 'grandmother' simply is 'a female whose child has a child,' and in natural identities, water simply is H_20. Similarly, so it is argued, to claim something is wrong is to claim that God prohibits it. The divine commands may be formatted as follows:

a. X is morally wrong = God prohibits X

b. Y is morally right = God commands Y

c. Z is morally neutral (neither good nor bad morally) = God neither commands nor prohibits Z

11

Why think this strong thesis might be true? It would anchor ethics in that which is beyond human culture. A divine command theory allows us to say that something is wrong even if a human culture approves of it. Also, this account seems to ground ethics at the very heart of reality. The purpose of ethics is intended by the Creator of the universe. H. P. Owen grants that while ethical precepts (keep promises, do not murder) seem like impersonal structures, they are best seen as personal commands.

[Moral] claims transcend every human person and every personal embodiment. On the other hand we value the personal more highly than the impersonal; so it is contradictory to assert that impersonal claims are entitled to the allegiance of our wills. The only solution to the paradox is to suppose that the order of [moral] claims, while it appears as impersonal from a purely moral point of view, is in fact rooted in the personality of God. (Owen 1965, 53)[15]

One difficulty is what might be called *the good atheist objection.* Aren't there atheists who grasp moral rightness and wrongness and act accordingly? This might not be decisive, however, because you might deny water is H_2O, and yet it is still constituted by hydrogen and oxygen. The deep structural foundation for ethics may not be evident to everyone who thinks ethically. And so the existence of ethical atheists is not, itself, a good objection to the strong divine command theory. But there is another problem: the Euthyphro Dilemma.

In the fourth century BCE Plato constructed a dialogue, the *Euthyphro*, which included a question that can be slightly re-phrased: Is X good because God loves it or is X loved by God because it is good. The problem with *X is good because of God's love* is that it then seems that love gives rise to reasons, and we may face this problem: what if God loved something unjust? If God loved cruelty, would cruelty then be right? Some have been prepared to go some of the way with this proposal and charge that if God did command cruelty, then it would be morally right and yet, (they argue) God did *not* command cruelty. This reasoning may suffice, but many philosophers worry about the coherence of someone (even God) making something morally right by decree or command. Commands can, under certain conditions, create new obligations as when someone who owns land offers a decree (imagine she prohibits hunting), but

15

we rarely think these commands can create obligations that are contrary to objective rights and wrongs. We would be uneasy with a landlord who could simply make murder right.

There is another version of the divine command theory that may be more successful. According to a moderate form of the theory for *X to be morally right* amounts to *X is commanded by an essentially good God*. On this view, goodness is not defined by Gods' commands. God is held to be good in God's self and the source of all goodness. In this framework murder is evil and compassion good, and necessarily so, but their necessary objective statues is derived from God's commands. This version of the divine command theory avoids the problem of caprice; God cannot, by God's very nature, command murder. But it still insists that these normative, objective truths stem from God.

Why should one adopt such a framework? It offers a unified, stable account of values as stemming from a single source. It makes no use of an appeal to God's sheer power; in other words, the obligatory nature of divine commands does not stem from an appeal to God's power, e.g. obey God or face intolerable consequences.

A difficulty with this theory arises in making clear the kind of causal relationships involved between God and objective moral norms. Causal relations are often thought to be contingent, but this is not always the case. Some determinists hold that *all* causal relations are fixed and Spinoza claimed that the whole cosmos could not be other than it is.

There is yet a third alternative that may be called Platonic theism which resembles the moderate divine command theory but does not claim that the objectivity of morality rests on God's commands. On this view, God is essentially good, and yet moral rightness or wrongness do not depend of God's commands. Nonetheless the very existence of a cosmos in which there are objective moral duties and values, rests upon God's causal creativity. The objectivity of morality, then, is not derived from God but the existence of a universe of moral beings is itself purposively willed by God. Morality and values have a *teleological structure*: their very existence and the ultimate fruition of the pursuit of values is part of God's intentional will.

13

If the strong version or moderate version of the divine command theory holds, then ethics and values do depend upon God. Given that God necessarily exists, the issue raised at the beginning of this chapter (if God does not exist, would everything be permissible?) would not arise because there is no possibility of God's nonexistence. If platonic theism turns out to be true, then ethics would have a cosmic intelligibility or purpose that naturalism would neither allow nor concede. Let us compare theistic and naturalistic ethics.

RELATION BETWEEN RELIGION AND ETHICS (HUMAN VALUES)

Man as a human being, cannot exist without religion because it is intrinsic in his nature. One cannot isolate religion from the life situation. Religion determines its true value from the role it plays in the enrichment of the quality of life. It has a role to play, a contributive role in the evolution of man, by providing society with ethical codes, social rules and ideals, rituals and devotion. Religion also enhances human values and Self-awareness.

Religion helps one to lead a disciplined and purified life. Religions always stand for the betterment of human soul. The different religions, though devotedly called by different names, show a surprising likeness of spirit and life. It is a unique specific expression and cannot be equated with anything. There is no religion which does not stress one form or other of universal brotherhood, and which does not advocate kindness to all living things. In the religions of the non-vegetarian people, there is an acceptance, in principle at least, of the non-killing commandment. And there is the general acceptance by the Semitic religions that a form of grace accompanies fasting and abstention from meat eating on certain days (Nataraga Guru *The Word of the Guru* 321)[16]. Buddhism in principle is solidly based on non-hurting (*ahimsa*), and Jainism makes the high level of this principle.

A religion worth the name must incorporate some system of morality for the guidance of its followers. The problem of the relationship between religion and ethics has occupied for sometimes an important place in the discourses of philosophers. The logical position regarding the relationship of ethics and religion in general, the intimate relationship between these two, as contingent facts of history, has never been, and can never be, denied.

Ethics is the study and evaluation of human conduct in the light of moral principles. Philosophers consider ethics as a philosophy. Some philosophers seek an absolute ethical criterion in religion. Major religions have stressed the importance of ethics. Religion, ethics and philosophy are interconnected. Religious vision gives necessary guidance to all other pursuits. Also ethical conduct and philosophical knowledge help the development of spirituality. Without ethics and philosophy religion becomes empty and in the same way without religious guidance, ethical and

---

[16] Guru, Nataraja. (1968). *The Word of the Guru*. Ernakulam: Paico Publishing House. P. 321

philosophical endeavours become meaningless. All religions recognize the importance of ethics. Religion as an encounter with something in the higher order of existence and morality as a personal and social code of conduct are interconnected; they constitute the spiritual endeavours of man.

Religion is concerned with the moral life of man. F.H. Bradly considers that religion is an expression of moral goodness of man. Bradly defines "Religion is rather the attempt to express the complete Reality of goodness through the very aspect of our being" (Paul Edwards 140)[17]. Apprehending religion from the angle of morality, N.F.S. Ferre says: "Religion is a search for power to overcome the evil side of life even more than its concern for understanding what life at its centre or depth means" (Y. Masih 3[18]).

The concept of free-will is a moral, religious and social concept that is central to most religions. It has been argued that the basis of freedom lies in the contingency of natural events. According to Kant, freedom of the will is the chief postulate of moral philosophy, it does not require proof, and it is an apriori truth (Kant, 18). Freedom is the very basis of morality. The moral and religious life is a genuine one, and it cannot be so without freedom. As far as the religious interpretation of the problem of the free-will is concerned, it seems that the religious traditions of the East and the West both have treated it very differently. Western religious traditions, especially Judaism and Christianity, deal with theproblem of free-will in two different spheres of philosophy; first the philosophy of religion and secondly the moral philosophy. In the philosophy of religion the problem of free-will arises in the context of theistic concept of good and evil. There, this is known as problem of evil. In morality, this is related to the human responsibility and comes as a problem of free-will and determinism.

Indian religious traditions are very much concerned with the concept of freedom, liberation and salvation, etc. Indian thinkers have discussed the problem of free-will and determinism under the heading 'law of *karma*'. The cosmic principle of *karma* conjoined with the universal law of causation, shapes itself into the Indian doctrine of *karma*, as every cause gives rise to an effect, so every action produces a result. Thus the doctrine of *karma* is not a dogmatic theory; rather, it is only an ethical version of the scientific law of causation. Radhakrishnan has described the

---

[17] Edwards, Paul., ed. (1967). *The Encyclopedia of Philosophy*. New York: Oxford University Press. P.140
[18] Masih, Y. (1991). *Introduction to Religious Philosophy*. Delhi: Motilal Banaesidass Publishers. P.3

doctrine of *karma* as "The law of *karma* is the counter-part in the moral world of the physical law of uniformity (S.Radhakrishnan *Indian Philosophy* 244)[19].

Sankaracharya accepted the principle of *karma*. He says, individuality is due to *karma*, whish is a product of *avidya*. Freedom from the subjection to the law of *karma* is the end of human life. To get rid of *avidya* is to be freed from the law of *karma*. The law of *karma* expresses the will of God. The order of *karma* is set up by God, who is the ruler of *karma*. Since the law is dependent on God's nature, God himself may be regarded as rewarding the righteous and punishing the wicked. To show that the law of *karma* is not independent of God, it is sometimes said that, though God suspends the law of *karma*, still he does not have the will to do so (S. Radhakrishnan *Indian Philosophy* 595[20]).

[19] Radhakrishnan, S. (1966). *Indian Philosophy*. 2 vols. 2nd ed. New York: Humanities Press. P. 244
[20] Radhakrishnan, S. (1966). *Indian Philosophy*. 2 vols. 2nd ed. New York: Humanities Press. P.595

THE UNIVERSAL DECLARATION OF GLOBAL ETHICS

Introduction

Humans tend to group themselves in communities with similar understandings of the meaning of life and how to act accordingly. For the most part, in past history such large communities, called cultures or civilizations, have tended on the one hand to live unto themselves, and on the other to dominate and, if possible, absorb the other cultures they encountered. For example, Christendom, Islam, China.

THE MEANING OF RELIGION (IDEOLOGY)

At the heart of each culture is what is traditionally called a Religion, that is: "An explanation of the ultimate meaning of life, and how to live accordingly." Normally all religions contain the four "C's": Creed, Code, Cult, Community-structure, and are based on the notion of the Transcendent.

- **Creed** refers to the cognitive aspect of a religion; it is everything that goes into the "explanation" of the ultimate meaning of life.
- **Code** of behavior or ethics includes all the rules and customs of action that somehow follow from one aspect or another of the Creed.
- **Cult** means all the ritual activities that relate the follower to one aspect or other of the Transcendent, either directly or indirectly, prayer being an example of the former and certain formal behavior toward representatives of the Transcendent, like priests, of the latter.
- **Community-structure** refers to the relationships among the followers; this can vary widely, from a very egalitarian relationship, as among Quakers, through a "republican" structure like Presbyterians have, to a monarchical one, as with some Hasidic Jews visa-vis their "Rebbe."

The Transcendent, as the roots of the word indicate, means "that which goes beyond" the every-day, the ordinary, the surface experience of reality. It can refer to spirits, gods, a Personal God, an Impersonal God, Emptiness, etc.

Especially in modern times there have developed "explanations of the ultimate meaning of life, and how to live accordingly" which are not based on a notion of the Transcendent, e.g., secular humanism, Marxism. Although in every respect these "explanations" function as religions traditionally have in human life, because the idea of the Transcendent, however it is understood, plays such a central role in religion, but not in these "explanations," for the sake of accuracy it is best to give these "explanations" not based on notion of the Transcendent a separate name; the name often used is: Ideology. Much, though not all, of the following will, mutatis mutandis, also apply to Ideology even when the term is not used.

NEED FOR A GLOBAL ETHIC

When the fact of the epistemological revolutions leading to the growing necessity of interreligious, interideological, intercultural dialogue is coupled with the fact of all humankind's interdependency--such that any significant part of humanity could precipitate the whole of the globe into a social, economic, nuclear, environmental or other catastrophe--there arises the pressing need to focus the energy of these dialogues on not only how humans perceive and understand the world and its meaning, but also on how they should act in relationship to themselves, to other persons, and to nature, within the context of reality's undergirding, pervasive, overarching source, energy and goal, however understood. In brief, humankind increasingly desperately needs to engage in a dialogue on the development of, not a Buddhist ethic, a Christian ethic, a Marxist ethic, etc., but of a global ethic--and I believe a key instrument in that direction will be the shaping of a UNIVERSAL DECLARATION OF A GLOBAL ETHIC.

I say ethic in the singular rather than ethics in the plural, because what is needed is not a full blown global ethics in great detail--indeed, such would not even be possible--but a global consensus on the fundamental attitude toward good and evil and the basic and middle principles to put it into action. Clearly also, this ethic must be global. It will not be sufficient to have a common ethic for Westerners or Africans or Asians, etc. The destruction, for example, of the ozone layer or the loosing of a destructive gene mutation by any one group will be disastrous for all. I say also that this UNIVERSAL DECLARATION OF A GLOBAL ETHIC must be arrived at by consensus through dialogue. Attempts at the imposition of a unitary ethics by various kinds of force have been had aplenty, and they have inevitably fallen miserably short of globality. The most recent failures can be seen in the widespread collapse of communism, and in an inverse way in the resounding rejection of secularism by resurgent Islamism.

That the need for a global ethic is most urgent is becoming increasingly apparent to all; humankind no longer has the luxury of letting such an ethic slowly and haphazardly grow by itself, as it willy-nilly will gradually happen. It is vital that there be a conscious focusing of energy on such a development. Immediate action is necessary:

    a. Every scholarly institution, whether related to a religion or ideology or not, needs to press its experts of the widest variety of disciplines to use their creativity among themselves and in conjunction with scholars from other institutions, both religiously related and not, in formulating a Global Ethic.

    b. Every major religion and ethical group needs to commission its expert scholars to focus their research and reflection on articulating a Global Ethic from the perspective of their religion or ethical group--in dialogue with all other religions and ethical groups.

c. Collaborative "Working Groups," of scholars in the field of ethics which are very deliberately interreligious, interideological need to be formed specifically to tackle this momentous task, and those which already exist need to focus their energies on it.

d. Beyond that there needs to be a major permanent Global Ethic Research Center, which will have some of the best experts from the world's major religions and ethical groups in residence, perhaps for years at a stretch, pursuing precisely this topic in its multiple ramifications.

When the UNIVERSAL DECLARATION OF A GLOBAL ETHIC is finally drafted--after multiple consultation, revision and eventual acceptance by the full range of religious and ethical institutions--it will then serve as a minimal ethical standard for humankind to live up to, much as the United Nation's 1948 Universal Declaration of Human Rights. Through the former, the moral force of the world's religious and ethical institutions can be brought to bear especially on those issues which are not very susceptible to the legal and political force of the latter. Such an undertaking by the Religions and Ideologies of the world would be different from, but complementary to, the work of the United Nations.

After the initial period, which doubtless would last several years, the "Global Ethic Research Center" could serve as an authoritative religious and ideological scholarly locus to which always-new specific problems of a global ethic could be submitted for evaluation, analysis and response. The weightiness of the responses would be "substantive," not "formal." That is, its solutions would carry weight because of their inherent persuasiveness coming from their intellectual and spiritual insight and wisdom.

PRINCIPLES OF A UNIVERSAL DECLARATION OF A GLOBAL ETHIC
Let me first offer some suggestions of the general notions that I believe ought to shape a UNIVERSAL DECLARATION OF GLOBAL ETHIC, and then offer a tentative draft constructed in their light:

I. The Declaration should use language and images that are acceptable to all major religions and ethical groups; hence, its language ought to be "humanity-based," rather than from authoritative religious books; it should be from "below," not from "above."

II. Therefore, it should be anthropo-centric, indeed more, it must be anthropo-cosmocentric, for we cannot be fully human except within the context of the whole of reality.

III. The affirmations should be dynamic in form in the sense that they will be susceptible to being sublated (aufgehoben), that is, they might properly be reinterpreted by being taken up into a larger framework.

IV. The Declaration needs to set inviolable minimums, but also open-ended maximums to be striven for; but maximums may not be required, for it might violate the freedom minimums of some persons.

V.   It could well start with--though not limit itself to-- elements of the so-called "Golden Rule": Treat others as we would be treated.

EXCURSUS: THE "GOLDEN RULE"

A glimpse of just how pervasive the "Golden Rule" is, albeit in various forms and expressions, in the world's religions and ideologies, great and small, can be garnered from this partial listing:

1) Perhaps the oldest recorded version--which is cast in a positive form--stems from Zoroaster (628-551 B.C.E.): "That which is good for all and any one, for whomsoever-- that is good for me...what I hold good for self, I should for all. Only Law Universal is true Law" (Gathas, 43.1).

2) Confucius (551-479 B.C.E.), when asked "Is there one word which may serve as a rule of practice for all one's life?" said: "Do not to others what you do not want done to yourself" (Analects, 12.2 & 15.23). Confucius also stated in a variant version: "What I do not wish others to do to me, that also I wish not to do to them" (Analects, 5.11).

3) The founder of Jainism was Vardhamana, known as Mahavira ("Great Hero--540-468 B.C.E.); the various scriptures of Jainism, however, derived from a later period: "A man should wander about treating all creatures as he himself would be treated" (Sutrakritanga 1.11.33). "One who you think should be hit is none else but you.... Therefore, neither does he cause violence to others nor does he make others do so" (Acarangasutra 5.101-2).

4) The founder of Buddhism was Siddhartha Gautama, known as the Buddha ("Enlightened One"--563-483 B.C.E.); the various scriptures of Buddhism also derived from a later period: "Comparing oneself to others in such terms as `Just as I am so are they, just as they are so am I,' he should neither kill nor cause others to kill" Sutta Nipata 705). "Here am I fond of my life, not wanting to die, fond of pleasure and averse from pain. Suppose someone should rob me of my life.... If I in turn should rob of his life one fond of his life.... How could I inflict that upon another?" (Samyutta Nikaya v.353).

5) The Hindu epic poem, the 3rd-century B.C.E. Mahabharata, states that its "Golden Rule," which is expressed in both positive and negative form, is the summary of all Hindu teaching, "the whole Dharma": "Vyasa says: Do not to others what you do not wish done to yourself; and wish for others too what you desire and long for for yourself- -this is the whole of Dharma; heed it well" (Mahabharata, Anusasana Parva 113.8).

6) In the biblical book of Leviticus (composed in the fifth century B.C.E., though some of its material may be more ancient) the Hebrew version of the "Golden Rule" is stated positively: "You shall love your neighbor as yourself" (Lev. 19: 18).

7) The deuterocanonical biblical Tobit was written around the year 200 B.C.E. and contains a negative version--as most are--of the "Golden Rule": "Never do to anyone else anything that you would not want someone to do to you" (Tobit 4:15).

8) The major founder of Rabbinic Judaism, Hillel, who lived about a generation before Jesus, though he may also have been his teacher, taught that the "Golden Rule"--his version being both positive and negative-- was the heart of the Torah; "all the rest was

commentary": "Do not do to others what you would not have done to yourself" (Btalmud, Shabbath 31a).

9) Following in this Jewish tradition, Jesus stated the "Golden Rule" in a positive form, saying that it summed up the whole Torah and prophets: "Do for others just what you want them to do for you" (Luke 6:31); "Do for others what you want them to do for you: this is the meaning of the Law of Moses [Torah] and of the teachings of the prophets" (Matthew 7:12).

10) In the seventh century of the Common Era Mohammed is said to have claimed that the "Golden Rule" is the "noblest Religion": "Noblest Religion is this-- that you should like for others what you like for yourself; and what you feel painful for yourself, hold that as painful for all others too." Again: "No man is a true believer unless he desires for his brother that which he desires for himself."

11) The "Golden Rule" is likewise found in some non-literate religions as well: "One going to take a pointed stick to pinch a baby bird should first try it on himself to feel how it hurts"

12) The eighteenth-century Western philosopher Immanuel Kant came up with a "rational" version of the "Golden Rule" in his famous "Categorical Imperative," or "Law of Universal Fairness": "Act on maxims which can at the same time have for their object themselves as universal laws of nature.... Treat humanity in every case as an end, never as a means only."

13) The late nineteenth-century founder of Baha'ism, Baha'ullah, wrote: "He should not wish for others that which he doth not wish for himself, nor promise that which he doth not fulfill."

14) In 1915 a new version of Buddhism, Won Buddhism, was founded in Korea by the Great Master Sotaesan. In the teachings he left behind are found variants of the "Golden Rule": "Be right yourself before you correct others. Instruct yourself first before you teach others. Do favors for others before you seek favors from them." "Ordinary people may appear smart in doing things only for themselves, but they are really suffering a loss. Buddhas and Bodhisattvas may appear to be stupid in doing things only for others, but eventually they benefit themselves."

It is clear that the core of the world's major Religions, the "Golden Rule," "does not attempt the futile and impossible task of abolishing and annihilating the authentic ego. On the contrary, it tends to make concern for the authentic ego the measure of altruism. `Do not foster the ego more than the alter; care for the alter as much as for the ego.' To abolish egoism is to abolish altruism also; and vice versa."

RELIGIOUS AND HUMAN VALUES AND THE SANCTITY OF LIFE DURING WAR

Introduction

World religions make use of the scripture to justify their actions, which are ultimately deployed in the context of war and peace (Almond 45). It is arguably evident that scriptural passages have been quoted as the guiding principles for the engagement in warfare and the establishment of peace. This implies that scriptural knowledge is vital when analyzing the religious values on war and peace, especially in societies whereby religion is used as a motivation and justification of war and peace (Daryl, 2010). This paper bases on comparative religious studies in order to have a comprehensive overview of the justifications for war and peace basing on the religious scriptures. The fundamental argument that forms the basis of the paper is that all religions in the world have within themselves the seeds that can be result to the establishment of either war or peace. It is also vital to take into account the viewpoint that factors that determine peace and war in the world religions are based on the divine commandments, teachings attained from the scriptures and the divine interpretations of the scriptures by the believers (Gopin, 2000). Basing on the scriptural comparisons of the various world religions, this paper discusses their respective religious views with regard to the elements of war and peace.

Consensus

A consensus among all the world religions in relation to war and peace is the opposition to use of force that is deemed lethal or killing. There are exceptional cases where killing and the use of force is justified, but only under particular circumstances (Hertog, 2006). A comparative review of the scriptures of the various world religions reveals that there is a fundamental rule against killing although there is a variation relating to the strength of the applicability of the rules.

In the context of Buddhism, every person usually trembles during the times of violence owing to the fact that life is cherished by every individual. According to Dhammapada 10.130, putting oneself in the place of another individual, a person is not required to kill. In addition, an individual is not required to compel another person to kill (Super 145).

Christianity

With regard to Christianity, killing is condemned in the bible. Matthew 5:21-22 clearly states that "thou shall not kill; and whoever kills will be in danger of judgment..." This clearly indicates the stance of killing with regard to the taking of another person's life (Irving 147). It is believed that an individual has no authority of taking another person's life.

Hinduism

Hinduism also lays emphasis on the respect for another person's life as a core requirement for the establishment of peace. As outlined in their scripture at Bhagavad Gita 16. 1-3, the supreme personality of Godhead outlines three transcendental individual qualities including fearlessness, having self-control, nonviolence, having a compassion for all living things and being free of anger (Hertog 96). These qualities are needed for the development of divine nature. In addition, their stance against violence is emphasized by the fact that the religion is against the use of attacks, even for those who are deemed most despicable. Furthermore, attacks should not be directed at those who are peace-making (Daryl 78).

Islam, Jainism, and Judaism

Islam is also against the taking of human life, which they perceive as made sacred by Allah, except in circumstances that call for just cause. This is stated in the Quran 17:33, and indicates the stance of the Muslims against killing. Jainism is also against the use of violence and people should avoid being involved violence as much as possible (Hertog 102). From its scriptures, Purushyartha Siddhyapaya 60, states that "having precisely understood the meaning of violence, its outcomes, the victims and the executor, individuals who embrace the values of the religion should restrain from violence, to the best of their capacity. The guiding principles of Judaism are somewhat similar to those held by the Christian faith; the doctrine prohibits individuals from committing murder, as stated in Exodus 20:13 (Gopin 125).

It is arguably evident that all the world religions oppose the taking of another person's life, which has been emphasized using commandments for the Abrahamic religions; moral standards and virtue in the case of Buddhism; and an advocacy for the establishment of peace and non violent activities in the case of Sikhism. Jainism does not have any exceptions and killing is prohibited for all forms of life (Gopin 126).

Causes that can give good reason for the use of armed force

In cases whereby force is deployed, all the world religions except for Jainism attempt to rationalize the use of armed force for just causes. Jainism emphasizes on the rule of non-killing. The different religions in the world have diverse conditions and scenarios that justify the use of force, with an emphasis on just causes and right motives. In the context of Buddhism, killing is only justified when protecting the Dharma by the kings, lay men and the upasakas as outlined in Mahaparinirvana Sutra, Chapter 5. Hinduism justifies the use of killing basing on the religious duty of fighting (Daryl 100). Armed force is also justified in Buddhism when an individual's life is threatened, for the case of self- defense and protecting the people. Hinduism prohibits the use of war for the purpose of conquest and a person has the authority of killing an assassin who has shown his/her intents of murder, such an acts results to no guilt, which is justified by their scriptures that state that " fury recoils upon fury" as outline sin the Manu Smrti 8.348-350. In addition, armed force is justified in cases whereby a person is administering punishment to a person who rightly deserves the punishment, provided that they are under the due process of justice (Hertog 148).

Islam justifies the use of armed force when fighting for the cause of Allah. However, limits are not supposed to be transgressed because they are prohibited in Quran 2:190 (Irving 145). Armed force is also justified to ensure that there is prevalence of justice and faith in the context of Allah. Fighting is also justified for defending one-self. The religion of Jainism does not justify any sort of killing whatsoever. Judaism on the other hand justifies killing for just causes of the Lord, as evident in Numbers 32:20-22. Justification also bases on penalty for taking someone else's life vests on the life of the killer; that is life for life and an eye for an eye (Almond 147).

It is arguably evident that the justifications for the use of armed forces and fighting are many including protecting the religion and righteousness, as the case of Buddhism, Hinduism, Islam and Judaism; protecting the innocents, as in the case of Hinduism and Islam; fighting to end oppression, as in the case of Islam and Sikhism; administering punishment to the performers of evil, which is the case of Christianity and Islam; self defense as in the case for Hinduism and Islam and acquisition of the promised land of God for Judaism. Jainism on the other hand does not justify any form of killing, even for the case defending one-self and protecting other people (Gopin 100). It is also important to note that self-defense is not viewed widely as a religious cause, resulting to its rejection in some religious scriptures such as the New Testament (Hertog 147).

The intent motive behind using force
The motive underlying the deployment of force is also an important aspect outlined in the doctrines of the various religions in relation to war and peace (Daryl 47). Even in cases where there is a justification of the cause, the values of most religions emphasize on the view that armed action must be undertaken with the true motives and attitudes. A comparative scriptural analysis reveals that Buddhism and Christianity stress on the importance of love and compassion for the enemies and those individuals who are receiving punishment. In the context of Hinduism, proper motive is determined by the undertaking of one's duty; this implies that using violence with wrong motives and unjustified killing results to negative consequences on oneself, as outlined in the principle of Karma (Gopin 78). The Muslim scripture outline the consequences of not acting with the right intent, which includes hell for any person who kills a believer purposefully. In the religious values of Islam and other religions such as Judaism, the right intent should aim at the fulfillment of the will of God. Sikhism on the other hand encourages their fighters not take think of their own lives and that self-sacrifice is case of martyrs. Jainism does not justify any intent for the case of killing, and a thought about killing constitutes a sin (Irving 74).

With regard to the authority to use force, Buddhism gives the king the power to punish. Christianity on the other hand gives the ruler the power of the sword and considers it as a right that is God ordained. Hinduism authorizes the kings and warriors to use armed forces when in a righteous battle. The Quran on the other hand lays emphasis on the going to war for the cause of Allah; it does not offer authority to specific people to wage war. Such authorities are allocated to the imams and Muslim leaders (Gopin 78). When deploying force as the last option, Buddhism lays emphasis on the soft approach, Christianity emphasizes on forgiveness, while Islam states that those in the quest for peace shall receive peace while those engaging treason shall be thrown back.

Conclusion

This paper has discussed the values of various religions towards war and peace. It is arguably evident that engaging in war needs a strong justification and that taking human life is only permitted under specific scenarios for important causes outlined in the doctrines. A general consensus across all the world religions is the opposition towards taking another person's life. The religious scriptures offer an important indication on the levels to which war and violence are embraced in a particular religion. The limitation is that it is subject to different interpretations, which has resulted to misrepresentation of the religious values relating to war and peace.

RELIGIOUS AND HUMAN VALUES: THE CASE OF THE GENEVA CONVENTIONS OF 1949

Introduction

The Geneva Conventions and their Additional Protocols are international treaties that contain the most important rules limiting the barbarity of war. They protect people who do not take part in the fighting (civilians, medics, aid workers) and those who can no longer fight (wounded, sick and shipwrecked troops, prisoners of war).

The Geneva Conventions and their Additional Protocols are at the core of international humanitarian law, the body of international law that regulates the conduct of armed conflict and seeks to limit its effects. They specifically protect people who are not taking part in the hostilities (civilians, health workers and aid workers) and those who are no longer participating in the hostilities, such as wounded, sick and shipwrecked soldiers and prisoners of war. The Conventions and their Protocols call for measures to be taken to prevent or put an end to all breaches. They contain stringent rules to deal with what are known as "grave breaches". Those responsible for grave breaches must be sought, tried or extradited, whatever nationality they may hold.

The 1949 Geneva Conventions

1. The first Geneva Convention protects wounded and sick soldiers on land during war.

This Convention represents the fourth updated version of the Geneva Convention on the wounded and sick following those adopted in 1864, 1906 and 1929. It contains 64 articles. These provide protection for the wounded and sick, but also for medical and religious personnel, medical units and medical transports. The Convention also recognizes the distinctive emblems. It has two annexes containing a draft agreement relating to hospital zones and a model identity card for medical and religious personnel.

2. The second Geneva Convention protects wounded, sick and shipwrecked military personnel at sea during war.

This Convention replaced Hague Convention of 1907 for the Adaptation to Maritime Warfare of the Principles of the Geneva Convention. It closely follows the provisions of the first Geneva Convention in structure and content. It has 63 articles specifically applicable to war at sea. For example, it protects hospital ships. It has one annex containing a model identity card for medical and religious personnel.

3. The third Geneva Convention applies to prisoners of war.

This Convention replaced the Prisoners of War Convention of 1929. It contains 143 articles whereas the 1929 Convention had only 97. The categories of persons entitled to prisoner of war status were broadened in accordance with Conventions I and II. The conditions and places of captivity were more precisely defined, particularly with regard to the labour of prisoners of war, their financial resources, the relief they receive, and the judicial proceedings instituted against them. The Convention establishes the principle that prisoners of war shall be released and repatriated without delay after the cessation of active hostilities. The Convention has five annexes containing various model regulations and identity and other cards.

4. The fourth Geneva Convention affords protection to civilians, including in occupied territory.

The Geneva Conventions, which were adopted before 1949. were concerned with combatants only, not with civilians. The events of World War II showed the disastrous consequences of the absence of a convention for the protection of civilians in wartime. The Convention adopted in 1949 takes account of the experiences of World War II. It is composed of 159 articles. It contains a short section concerning the general protection of populations against certain consequences of war, without addressing the conduct of hostilities, as such, which was later examined in the Additional Protocols of 1977. The bulk of the Convention deals with the status and treatment of protected persons, distinguishing between the situation of foreigners on the territory of one of the parties to the conflict and that of civilians in occupied territory. It spells out the obligations of the Occupying Power vis-à-vis the civilian population and contains detailed provisions on humanitarian relief for populations in occupied territory. It also contains a specific regime for the treatment of civilian internees. It has three annexes containing a model agreement on hospital and safety zones, model regulations on humanitarian relief and model cards.

Common Article 3

Article 3, common to the four Geneva Conventions, marked a breakthrough, as it covered, for the first time, situations of non-international armed conflicts. These types of conflicts vary greatly. They include traditional civil wars, internal armed conflicts that spill over into other States or internal conflicts in which third States or a multinational force intervenes alongside the government. Common Article 3 establishes fundamental rules from which no derogation is permitted. It is like a mini-Convention within the Conventions as it contains the essential rules of the Geneva Conventions in a condensed format and makes them applicable to conflicts not of an international character:

- ❖ It requires humane treatment for all persons in enemy hands, without any adverse distinction. It specifically prohibits murder, mutilation, torture, cruel, humiliating and degrading treatment, the taking of hostages and unfair trial.
- ❖ It requires that the wounded, sick and shipwrecked be collected and cared for.
- ❖ It grants the ICRC the right to offer its services to the parties to the conflict.

- ❖ It calls on the parties to the conflict to bring all or parts of the Geneva Conventions into force through so-called special agreements.
- ❖ It recognizes that the application of these rules does not affect the legal status of the parties to the conflict.
- ❖ Given that most armed conflicts today are non-international, applying Common Article 3 is of the utmost importance. Its full respect is required.

States Party to the Geneva Conventions

The Geneva Conventions entered into force on 21 October 1950. Ratification grew steadily through the decades: 74 States ratified the Conventions during the 1950s, 48 States did so during the 1960s, 20 States signed on during the 1970s, and another 20 States did so during the 1980s. Twenty-six countries ratified the Conventions in the early 1990s, largely in the aftermath of the break-up of the Soviet Union, Czechoslovakia and the former Yugoslavia.

Seven new ratifications since 2000 have brought the total number of States Party to 194, making the Geneva Conventions universally applicable.

THE UNIVERSAL ROLE OF RELIGION IN SOCIAL LIFE

Introduction

Every society has a dominant culture, usually with religious roots. Secularization reflected a move away from religion as a dominant source of social mores in the western world. As well, it is characterized by the rise of individualism, where the individual is more important than the community.

Religion and human dignity

Religion is a fundamental part of human dignity. For many adherents, it is far more than a mere lifestyle choice, it is the deepest part of who they are. To violate a person's religious freedom or require them to act against their religious beliefs or practices violates the very core of that person's being (Charles Taylor, 1995). Sociological studies have shown positive benefits of religious affiliation for school performance, positive family life, well-being and contribution to community life. Religions also provide for rites of passage such as marking birth, marriage and death (E.H. Schludermann, S. Schludermann and C. Huynh, 2000).

Ethical laws/ fostering moral government/ religious institutions and humanitarian works

According to Winnifred Fallers Sullivan (1994), religions generally promote ethical, law-abiding behaviour in their adherents. Religious adherents strive to obey the law and respect the authority of the state. Religion thereby fosters "moral self-government." Kelsay and Twiss (1994) argue, "Cooperation, sharing, and altruism can all be related to the sense of identity that religious traditions provide." Religious institutions are the source of much humanitarian work internationally including Ghana. Religious adherents provide much of the funding as well as volunteer labour for these institutions (Statistics Canada, 2004). However, "these traditions suffer a loss of function when they are removed from the domain of public life."

What happens if they are denigrated?

It appears, then, that if religious adherence is valued and accommodated, the benefits that accrue to society are well-behaved citizens that contribute to the well-being of society. If religious adherence is denigrated, if it is marginalized, if it is shut out from public life, society will not only lose the benefits derived from religious adherents but also likely face a backlash from religious adherents.

Religion: make or break?

Opponents of religion like to focus on the divisive effects of religion; on conflict and wars occurring with religious overtones. In many other conflicts, however,

i.   Religion has been a positive force for peace and for state building. In Poland and East Germany, for example, civil society began in church basements (Douglas Johnston and Cynthia Sampson, 1994).

ii. In South Africa, a national day of prayer contributed to the relative peace in which the 1994 general election was held (Michael Cassidy, 1995).

Francis Fukuyama (1992) argues that religion is part of the "art of associating" that is necessary for the functioning of liberal democracy. Attachment to a religious community therefore facilitates engagement with and pride in democratic institutions.

Freedom of religion

Freedom of religion is a cornerstone of a free society. Chief Justice Dickson articulated the broad right to religious freedom in ringing terms in the first Supreme Court of Canada judgment on section 2(*a*) of the *Charter:*

> A truly free society is one which can accommodate a wide variety of beliefs, diversity of tastes and pursuits, customs and codes of conduct. A free society is one which aims at equality with respect to the enjoyment of fundamental freedoms.... Freedom must surely be founded in respect for the inherent dignity and the inviolable rights of the human person. The essence of the concept of freedom of religion is the right to entertain such religious beliefs as a person chooses, the right to declare religious beliefs openly and without fear of hindrance or reprisal, and the right to manifest belief by worship and practice or by teaching and dissemination (*R. v. Big M Drug Mart, 1985*).

The issue of secularism

These lofty words are inspiring but the reality is that religious teachings and practices often bump up against the prevailing secular society.

This raises the question of what is meant by "a secular society." Iain Benson (2000) helpfully developed a typology in a 2000 article titled "Notes Towards a (Re)Definition of the 'Secular'" to identify the various ways that a secular state can interact with religion within its borders:

1. *neutral secular*: The state is expressly non-religious and must not support religion in any way;
2. *positive secular*: The state does not affirm religious beliefs of any particular religion but may create conditions favourable to religions generally;
3. *negative secular*: The state is not competent in matters involving religion but must not act so as to inhibit religious manifestations that do not threaten the common good;

4. *inclusive secular*: The state must not be run or directed by a particular religion but must act so as to include the widest involvement of different faith groups, including non-religious.

There is thus not one, single understanding of the meaning of "secular" when it comes to the responsibilities of the state towards religion.

Conclusion

Simplistic answers do not suffice when addressing the place of religious observance, and religious accommodation, in a multi-religious, yet secular society. I would argue the inclusive secular approach should be used as the starting point; that maximum inclusion and accommodation of religious observance. Religion is deeply important to believers and should be respected wherever possible.

THE PROTESTANT ETHIC AND THE SPIRIT OF CAPITALISM

Introduction

Have you ever thought much about the economic system into which you were born? Would you say there was a 'spirit' that moves it? Sociologist Max Weber was fascinated by the influence of thoughts and beliefs in history, and particularly why religion seemed to be a significant factor in determining levels of wealth.

Weber noticed that in the Germany of his time, the business leaders and owners of capital, not to mention the bulk of higher skilled workers and managers, were Protestant as opposed to Catholic. Protestants also had higher levels of educational achievement. The conventional explanation was that, in the 16th and 17th centuries, particular towns and regions in Germany had thrown off the rule of the Catholic church, and in the sudden freedom from a repressive regime controlling every aspect of their lives they were able to pursue their economic interests and become prosperous.

In fact, Weber notes, it was the very laxness of the Church in terms of moral and societal rules that turned the bourgeois middle classes against it. These burghers actually welcomed a tyranny of Protestant control that would tightly regulate their attitudes and behavior. Weber's question was, why did the richer classes in Germany, Netherlands, Geneva and Scotland, and also the groups that became the American Puritans, want to move in this direction? Surely freedom and prosperity comes with less, not more, religious control?

The capitalist spirit

At the outset of this famous but short book, Weber admits that discussing the 'spirit' of capitalism seems pretentious. Forms of capitalism had, after all, existed in China, India, Babylon and the classical world, and they had had no special ethos driving them aside from trade and exchange.

It was only with the emergence of modern capitalism, he suggests, that a certain ethic grew linking moral righteousness with making money. It was not just that Protestants sought wealth more purposefully than Catholics, but that Protestants showed "a special tendency to develop economic rationalism", that is, a particular approach to creating wealth that was less focused on the gain of comfort than on the pursuit of profit itself. The particular satisfaction was not in the money extracted to buy things (which had always driven money-making in the past), but in 'wealth creation' based on increased productivity and better use of resources. Long after all needs had been met, the capitalist did not rest, forever seeking greater profit for its own sake and as the symbol of more profound ends.

Weber had studied non-Christian religions and their relationship to economics. He observed that Hinduism's caste system, for instance, would always be a big obstacle to the development of capitalism because people were not free to be professionally or socially mobile. The Hindu spiritual ethic was to attempt to transcend the world, an outlook not dissimilar to Catholicism's creation of monasteries and convents to remove the holy people from the sins and temptations of the world outside. The Protestant ethic, in contrast, involved living with your eyes on God but fully in the world.

The expression of spiritual energies through work and business obviously gave its believers tremendous economic advantage. Instead of being told that business was an inferior quest compared to the holy life, one could be holy through one's work. Capitalistic enterprise was transformed from being simply a system of economic organization, to a domain of life infused with God.

The Protestant difference

Weber is careful not to say that there was anything intrinsically better about the theology of Protestantism. Rather, the general outlook on life and work that the early Protestant sects – Calvinists, Methodists, Pietists, Baptists, Quakers - drew from their beliefs made them singularly well adapted to modern capitalism. They brought to it:

- A spirit of progress;
- A love of hard work for its own sake;
- Orderliness, punctuality and honesty;
- Hatred of time-wasting through socializing, idle talk, sleep, sex or luxury (expressed in the sentiment, "every hour lost is lost to labour for the glory of God");
- Attention to the most productive use of resources, represented by profit. ("You may labour to be rich for God, though not for the flesh and sin" said Calvinist Richard Baxter);
- Absolute control of self (emotions and body) and aversion to spontaneous enjoyment;
- Belief in calling, or "proving one's faith in worldly activity".

Many Calvinist writers had the same contempt for wealth that the Catholic ascetics did, but when you looked more closely at their writings, Weber noted, their contempt was for the enjoyment of wealth and the physical temptations that came with it. Constant activity could drive out such temptations, therefore work could be made holy. If it was where your spiritual energies could be expressed, then work could be your salvation.

Thus, the peculiar nature of the early Protestant capitalists emerged: famously focused on their business, and as a result highly successful – yet going to great lengths not to enjoy its fruit. Catholicism had always had a degree of guilt about business and money making, but unrestricted by a bad conscience the Puritan sects became known as reliable, trustworthy and eager to please in their business dealings. This combination of "intense piety with business acumen", as Weber describes it, became the cornerstone of many great fortunes.

Calling and capitalism

Weber argues that the idea of 'calling' only came in with the Protestant Reformation. Martin Luther had discussed it, but it took the Puritan sects to make it central to their way of life.

Calling was related to Protestant theologian Calvin's idea of 'predestination' – that you did not know while you were alive whether you were one of God's 'elect', that is, whether you would live in eternity or be eternally damned. Therefore, you had to appear to be one of the elect, and this meant leading a spotless, well-ordered life of extreme self-control. If you were successful in your work, it was a sign that you were one of the chosen.

This irrational, spiritual concept ironically gave rise to a very rational brand of economic activity. Two of its notable effects were the self-limiting of consumption and the "ascetic compulsion to save". The outcome, Weber notes, was that capital was freed up for systematic investment, making the rich even richer.

Final comments

Today, as Ghanaians, we criticize ourselves from being too much a consumerist society, buying and using instead of saving and creating. Weber is worth reading to be reminded of the true spirit of capitalism – that it is not actually about a mad rush to spend and consume, but the creation of wealth through good use of resources. Weber describes this outlook thus:

> "Man is only a trustee of the goods which have come to him through God's grace. He must, like the servant in the parable, give an account of every penny entrusted to him, and it is at least hazardous to spend any of it for a purpose which does not serve the glory of God but only one's enjoyment".

Yet he also noted that the modern capitalistic system that Puritanism had helped to create eventually lost its religious impulse. If you had a 'calling', it was a meaningful system which could release all your wonderful potential. However, if you did not, it could seem soulless and even oppressive, an 'iron cage'. There is always a gulf between people who are little concerned with the nature of the work they do as long as it brings in the money and gives them some social standing – and those who must feel that what their work must be fulfilling their potential. It is this group which continually breathes new life into economies and societies. If you have a calling or a sense of duty in the work you do then your performance naturally gains an extra, powerful dimension. With a calling, Weber told us, there was no problem at all in squaring up the spiritual and economic aspects of life.

The Protestant Ethic and the Spirit of Capitalism showed how character traits, strongly shaped by religion, could play a massive role in the creation of wealth. Yet these traits, as outlined in the dot points above, do not necessarily depend on a certain religion for their flowering, and can be witnessed the world over where economies have taken off. The Asian economies that have had such a spectacular economic rise over the last twenty years have only minor Protestant populations, but their industrious, conscientious citizens have much in common with the dutiful and self-denying burghers of 17th century Germany.[21]

---

[21] Weber, Max. (2001 [1930]). The Protestant Ethic and the Spirit of Capitalism. New York, NY: Routledge.

ISLAM, HUMANITY, AND HUMAN VALUES

Defining humanity

A definition of humanity seems easy to think of yet difficult to propose, and there have been disputes about it among different schools of thought. Most pioneers in social thought and leaders of movements claim that the main feature of their activities is their humanism and humanitarian efforts. To avoid having misconceptions about humanity or sinking in the whirlpool of literal interpretations and logical disputes, we need to first focus on the reality of the human being and his different aspects, and then discuss the derived infinitive word form *humanity*, its meaning, virtues, and functions.

1) First, human beings are objective beings who are different from other objective beings with respect to freedom of choice, meaning that their actions and behaviours are a result of their reasoning and will, albeit relatively.

2) Second, human beings are to a large extent affected by their surroundings, that is, the physical environment and other beings.

3) Third, human beings are social beings who naturally interact with other human beings.

4) Fourth, human beings are created by God, the Creator of the universe. This relation with God has different dimensions which affect them as persons and all of their relationships. These four features are like four chapters of the book of humanity. Thus, human values are those basic elements in the nature of human beings which are to be developed by his own efforts. This development is an evolutionary movement in which no part of the human existence harms the others and none of these elements should stop the movement of the human being towards a better state.

These are the outlines for his comprehensive perfection which originate from his very nature. Man's God-given nature and colour are like seeds and potentials which are hidden in him at the beginning of creation and will flourish when man follows the right path.

Alternative theories

1) **First Theory:** One theory is to deny the first aspect of a human being's nature and assume that the human being is a phenomenon in the whole creation like other phenomena. His freedom and freedom of choice are natural and determined. This theory was commonly believed among the French existentialists and Greek peripatetics.

2) **Second Theory:** A second theory is to exclude him from other natural creatures and assume him to be different in soul and body from the material world he lives in, but at the same time, 'subdued by his determined destiny'. This belief is widely held among determinists.

3) **Third Theory:** A third theory is to assume the human being as the one who is the base of the society and such a society is nothing but a collection of people. Some Jewish philosophers and radical delegators (*Mufawwiah*) have had ideas similar to this theory.
4) **Fourth Theory:** A fourth theory is to ignore the relation of God with the human being, disregard the human being's dimensions from the beginning to eternity, and ignore his relation with all other creatures in his creation, his role, and his destiny. This idea is held among the materialists and western philosophers who rose up against scholasticism and religious thoughts. Most socialists and contemporary philosophers believe that nothing beyond matter and metaphysics should have any influence on objective creatures.

If we accept one of these four theories, we will find ourselves against another type of humanity.

1. Islam and humanity

The holy Qur'an emphasizes on the full alignment of religion and humanity:

> **So set your heart on the religion as a people of pure faith, the origination of Allah according to which He originated mankind; There is no altering Allah's creation; that is the upright religion... (Q 30:30)**

Also, the following hadith suggests that Islam is in harmony with the human's nature: "All the born are born with the God-given nature."

When it is said that Islam means to surrender to God, it means whenever something or someone is put in its or his real position in creation, it or he will be a Muslim. Thus, the position for which God has created human being is to achieve humanity and the human being's humanity equals his Islam, i.e., his level of submission to God. A human being is related with God, his own kind, nature, and the whole creation from that natural position.

So, a human being's Islam is his humanity. The holy Qur'an emphasizes on the full alignment of religion and humanity. The following verses demonstrate this truth:

> **So if they believe in the like of what you believe in, then they are certainly guided; and if they turn away, then they are only [steeped] in defiance. Allah shall suffice you against them, and He is the All-hearing, the All-knowing. The baptism of Allah, and who baptizes better than Allah? And Him do we worship. (2:137-138)**

2. Who can define characteristics of man?

Defining man and his characteristics cannot be carried out by man himself. There are several reasons for this, the most important of which are listed below:

a. Firstly, people's understanding of themselves and their feelings is influenced by their social and cultural standpoints, their unique situations, and their worldly interests.

b. Secondly, people are at various stages of continued development and therefore, they never exactly understand existential dimensions of human beings as they progress and make efforts to reach them.

Thus, if a human being wants to define human dimensions, features and virtues, his definition will be limited or biased to some extent. This leads to a multiplicity of definitions of humanness which causes a human being's goals and purposes to go into a halo of imaginations. But, Allah (swt), the Creator of the human being and the entire universe, is the only Able One to define the human being's characteristics. These characteristics are, in fact, dimensions of one perfect humanity. This is the meaning of necessity of heavenliness, unseenness (*ghaybi*), and absoluteness of religion.

To emphasize on the truth of this issue, we need to refer to the opinions of Islamic scholars. We are also guided by principles such as 'legislative obligations are graceful indicators of intellectual obligations' and 'whatever judgement is made by reason is made by religion and vice versa.'

Thus, we can conclude that Islam is identical with humanity and human values and vice versa.

Impact of belief in One God

The basic of Islamic beliefs is to believe in one God who has the Most Beautiful names and noblest qualities; One who neither begets, nor was begotten. The belief in this core possesses several advantages:

a. Firstly, it frees the human being from full submission to (worshiping) any natural being or any human being of whatever position and rank, and this freedom saves him from being confined to any material limits.

b. Secondly, it results in mobilizing all human talents and power for one purpose and saves him from all that destroys his life and activities, such as polytheism, being spoiled, etc.

c. Thirdly, it leads a human being towards the infinite goal and carves a long and endless path for his ambitions in which he can progress from cradle to grave and even after death. Thus, death does not stop a human's progress towards goals, As mentioned in hadiths, the progress will continue with righteous children, compiling useful books and giving an on-going zakat. If one introduces a good practice to the society and one or more people follow it after one's death, he or she will become more complete and receive more rewards until the day of resurrection.

d. Fourthly, it will keep one away and safe from other people's troubles and objections so that infinity and immateriality will direct his efforts, activities, and acts of giving.

e. Fifth, it will mobilize collective power in a competitive harmony and will prevent collective polytheism in order to prevent the society from division and thereby wasting the power of its members. It is stated in the Qur'an: "*...and do not be among the polytheists of those who split up their religion and became sects...*" (30:31-32)

f.   Sixth, the meaning of *"He neither begat, nor was begotten"* (112:3) will eliminate the effect of personal elements and relations from human value-setting system, because people are equal like a comb's teeth. Everyone only possesses through his own efforts and no one else's.

The above-mentioned points prove the effect of belief in the resurrection and in God's justice, on people's thinking and views, regardless of whether the person is good or bad, and to whatever extent his goodness or badness is. Moreover, the effect of faith on these elements in knowing human values reflects the following points:

I.   First, the great position of humanity is to take the responsibility in all major and minor works, overt and covert activities. All spoken and unspoken words of a person render him responsible for all his deeds and thoughts. Responsibility is the effect of the human being upon himself and/or others. Thus, taking responsibility results in a high status for the person and it is the reason for his dignity.

II. Second, it generates a trust in the person's heart in that his visible and invisible efforts will not be wasted. It assures that if one's efforts are made sincerely, they will be accepted and rewarded, even if the desired result is not achieved due to an obstacle beyond the person's control. The Qur'an states in this regard:

> *"...And whoever leaves his home migrating toward Allah and His Apostle and is then overtaken by death, his reward shall certainly fall on Allah..."* (4:100).

Thus, a person who merely attempts to act with sincerity, Allah (swt) will undoubtedly reward him or her. Moreover, Islamic scholars agree upon the fact that even if one has unintentionally made a mistake while he is trying to achieve good deed, he will have a reward before God.

III. Third, it can be understood from the previous point that believing in resurrection facilitates carrying out a human being's duty in the progress of the society and his own progress in any circumstances. A believer would make an effort to achieve that great goal, regardless of the views of those who benefit from the current status of the society. Such a person seeks God's contentment and asks Him for rewards in this life and in the hereafter.

IV. Fourth, people must pay attention to the role of repentance in the reinforcement of human effort, keeping him away from despair and disappointment, and facilitating the making up of past errors.

Man is central in Islamic culture

Islam introduces general concepts based on human values and preserving them for the establishment of the original culture for Muslims and provides a comprehensive view towards the universe and life. One would understand the extent of humanism of Islam's view if he explores it with regards to the human being, life, the universe, society, and other general theoretical concepts unavailable in the domain of science and experience.

A human being is very honourable in the Qur'an and higher than many other creatures. He is created by the best Creator in the best form. He is created by God and chosen by Him to be His representative on earth. God has taught him the names and breathed into him of His spirit, ordered the angels to prostrate before the human being and disposed the sun, the moon, the stars, and the day and night for him. A human being is honoured with endless potential for knowledge and the only creature to whom God has granted the potential perfection of supremacy over universal forces and other creatures. A human being is a noble-natured creature who is guided to two ways of good and evil and is inspired with virtues and vices to become perfect in the struggle he is in with the help of his freedom of choice. This feature is exclusive to him among all creatures and this enables him to elevate higher than angels.

Islam's view about death, disease, and disasters is very compassionate and humane. Death is the ornament of life which is like a necklace around a girl's neck that beautifies her. It is themeans of testing human beings and it is a blessing that God tries us to determine which one of us does better deeds.

Death is a gateway to the All-forgiving God who has the best and most eternal things. Death is not the end of man's life. A human being can pass the bridge of death while he is happy with what he is given by God because, as he continues his life by divine sustenance, he is also being given good news about the comforts which he has not yet received. He can have eternal deeds and can eternalize his activities.

However, disease, disaster, and losing properties, people, and children are all tests for people which enable them to develop their talents and to practice patience as well as helping them learn about their real capacity and capabilities, since they belong to Allah and to Him they will return. As well, tragedies, diseases, and natural disasters can act as stimuli for knowing them, avoiding their disastrous consequences, and learning to control them to a possible extent. According to what has been mentioned above, they all create the divine school which makes human knowledge develop. In the Islamic view, the future belongs to pious people and victory belongs to God's friends and God wants the abased to inherit and lead the earth. The fruit of such a look is a positive feeling and believing in victory and success. The universe is a big altar where everything prostrates before God, praises Him, prays to Him, and seeks refuge before Him. Everything in this world is created based on order, size, and value. Such a view will have a positive effect on a human being's activities and efforts.

Society in Islam
The structure Islam proposes for the society of the faithful is among the most important cultural elements of Islam and is the most effective support for human values.

In Islam, society is to be a united body where conflict and ranking based on social class has no place. It consists of people having different skills and capabilities who at the same time are connected, exchange services, and collaborate with one other. Every one of these members becomes complete and grows through interaction and exchange with others. Society is made from them and for them. Thus, it is a model of a human being and not just made of one of a human's dimensions. It is not a model of one individual or social dimension. If only one of his dimensions improved, that dimension would become a means of dominance and considerable pressure over one specific dimension and would lead to the distortion of human's reality and disfiguring of his real face.

The society is a system formed of different kinds of people. In an Islamic society, no one has any advantage over another. No class has superiority over another, no race has any advantage over another, and no group has any advantage over another. Even the majority has no advantage over the minority or vice versa; the society is simply for the human being. Such a society is built for all people and it is not set up such that only some of man's dimensions and potentials grow. This society pays attention neither just to individualism and nor to social issues only such that it gives up on individual issues. It neither ignores the body nor the soul. Therefore, there is no monasticism in Islam. The society is equivalent to all people. It enables the improvement of their skills and provides the opportunity for everyone's positive capabilities to develop.

In the Islamic view, the difference and variety of nations in the world is to know each other to foster collaboration: this leads to the perfection of human beings in the world and nations' difference is exactly like people's difference in the society. The human being's dependence on the things around him or those belonging to him restrains him from feeling any form of superiority, whether it is racial, hierarchal, and so forth.

Nationality, tribe, and family are not worthy of worship and must not become like idols. One cannot develop one of them and ignore other people's interests as a result. Wealth, like other facilities, is available to people and it is not meant for ruling over anyone. ealth is a trust and gift from God for the benefit of mankind and therefore, what is the most fundamental is the human being and not wealth or means of production. Thus, in
Islamic economy, human resources are the primary and most important factor of production. The labour can share in the profit made without being liable to any loss, while the investor has liability for losses. Also, labour may have a fixed wage, but setting a fixed increment for the capital is considered as usury and is forbidden.

Islamic rulings in social economics are full of humanistic directions. At the same time, Islam tries to prevent money from controlling human beings or just remaining among the rich ones. With respect to dominance, Islam rejects any kind of natural or hereditary dominance of some people over others except the dominance of legitimate guardians over the weak and unable ones. The only legitimate dominance is the one that originates from God or is based on agreement and consensus of people themselves. Government is a trust and not a privilege.

Furthermore, when people entrust power to a government this will be valid only if all conditions of a contract are provided such as freedom of choice, maturity, and awareness. People must not be forced to choose a government or be misinformed about the performance of governors, etc.

An Islamic society is the one in which a very productive ground for preserving human values and their promotion exists.

Morality in Islam

Morality is the great goal of religious teachings and the main factor in forming a religion. In the Islamic moral system, there is a severe opposition to those factors that inhibit people from connecting with other creatures, such as fear, and those which prevent people from communicating and interacting with one another, such as cruelty, hard-heartedness, and vanity. These qualities cause a sense of self-sufficiency that prevents one from interacting with others. It also produces an arrogance that creates a barrier to receiving divine blessings and makes it difficult for others to benefit from an arrogant person. The Islamic moral system includes foundations of human values and the paths to achieve and preserve them.

Islamic rulings safeguard values

Islam does not ignore human needs. Nor does Islam ask people to ignore or oppose them. There is no monasticism in Islam. Islam considers the way and means of meeting such needs as divine blessings and fulfilling them with good intentions as worship. Islam has regulated and defined limits for meeting these needs so that all dimensions of a human being are considered and his capabilities are protected; otherwise, God has created all creatures on earth for human beings and rejects the inhibition of ornaments and the *halal* (permitted) sustenance He has created for them.

On the other hand, one can call the categorization of the abovementioned needs as permitted and prohibited as *Islamic mysticism* (*tasawwuf*). A person would not take a step to fulfil his needs unless he is sure of divine satisfaction about his act. In doing so, he would be kept safe from going astray by following his own desires, which are mostly reflections of the surrounding material world. In fact, this mysticism is completely different from the known mysticism which is based on disregarding all desires in order to purify the self and perfect the soul. This mysticism keeps the human being safe from getting used to follow his own desires and whims. The human being is asked to be active and effective in his environment rather than passive and to be the driving factor of development and promotion. Achieving this goal is not fulfilled by drowning in desires.

In addition to the cases and causes of permitted and prohibited issues in Islam, what is interesting is that Islam interprets the permissible as the pure and pleasant and the prohibited issues as loathsome. This shows that the human being by himself is considered as an honoured and pure being.

It is difficult to represent Islamic rulings and investigate their effects on preserving human values in this short paper. So, I suffice to bring some examples and end this discussion.

Acts of worship, obligations, and prohibitions are conditional upon one's power and ability. When severe distress and intolerable difficulties are involved, legal issues may be cancelled, and the same can be understood from the rule of negation of harming and being harmed. Unawareness, force, emergency, mistake, and forgetfulness can all be factors that absolve someone from responsibilities. Working is considered as an act of worship; so is communication and fulfilling family and social tasks in order to keep their sanctity and human-orientation.

Interactions among people and groups in all forms become humane and these issues are even demonstrated in rulings of war.

The items mentioned here are just examples of how Islam protects human concepts and values which I humbly offer here. I stress that fact that every headline of this article is by itself a topic in the holy Qur'an that can be studied separately and that the unity of Islam with humanity and human values confirms the expansion of this discussion. Indeed, it proves the necessity of investigating this topic in Islamic sciences in the form of a complete encyclopaedia. I hope that God, the One who established the legislation of Islam and created man, accepts this effort of mine which has a very little value in His presence.

REFERENCES:

1. Caprara, G. V., Schwartz, S. H., Cabaña, C., Vaccine, M., & Barbaranelli, C. (2005).
   a. Personality and politics: Values, traits, and political choice. *Political Psychology,*
2. Bardi, A. (2000). *Relations of values to behavior in everyday situations.* Unpublished
   a. doctoral dissertation. The Hebrew University.
3. Schwartz, S. H., & Boehnke, K. (2004). Evaluating the structure of human values with
   a. confirmatory factor analysis. *Journal of Research in Personality, 38,* 230-255.
4. P.H. Coetzee and A.P.J. Roux (1998). *The African Philosophy Reader.* London:
   Routledge.
5. Almond, Gabriel. (2003). *A String Religion.* Chicago: University of Chicago Press.
6. Daryl, Charles. (2010). *War, Peace, and Christianity: Questions and Answers from a
   Just-War Perspective.* New York: Crossway publications.
7. Gopin, Marc. (2000). *Between Eden and Armageddon: the future of world religions,
   violence, and peacemaking.* Oxford: Oxford University Press.
8. Kalyvas, Stathis. (1996). *The rise of Christian Democracy in Europe.* Ithaca, NY: Cornell
   University Press
9. Iannaccone, Laurence. (1991). The consequences of religious market structure. Adam
   Smith and the economics of religion. *Rationality and Society, 3,* 156-177.
10. Almond, Gabriel A., & Powell, G. Bingham, Jr. (1978). *Comparative politics. System,
    process, and policy* (2nd rev. ed.). Boston: Little, Brown.
11. Johnson, J.T. (2004). "From Moral Norm to Criminal Code: The Law of Armed Conflict
    and the Restraint of Contemporary War." In A. Lang, Jr., A.C. Pierce & J.H. Rosenthal
    (eds.), *Ethics and the Future of Conflict: Lessons from the 1990s.* New Jersey: Prentice
    Hall Publishers.
12. Reichberg, G., Syse, H. &Begby, E. (eds.) (2006). *The Ethics of War: Classic and
    Contemporary Readings.* Oxford: Blackwell Publishing.
13. Darrin P Dixon. (2007). "The Role of Religious Values in Politics" *Race, Religion and
    the Law.* Available at: http://works.bepress.com/darrin_dixon/2/
14. Adler, F. (1956). The Value Concept in Sociology. American Journal of Sociology, 62:7.

15. Thurstone, L. L. (1959). The Measurement of Values. Chicago: The University of Chicago Press.

16. Wickert, F. (1940). A Test for Personal Goal Values. Journal of Social Psychology,
17. 11:15.

18. Ayers, A. J. (1952). Language, Truth & Logic.New York: Dover Publications.

19. Kroeber, A. L. (1952). The Nature of Culture. Chicago University of Chicago Press.

20. Kroeber, A. L., and C. Kluckhohn. (1963). Culture: A Critical Review of Concepts and Definitions. In Papers of the Peabody Museum of American Archaeology and Ethnology, edited by Alfred A. Knopf. New York: Vintage Edition.

21. England, G. W., and R. Lee. (1974). The Relationships between Managerial Values, Success in USA, Japan, India and Australia.Journal of Applied Psychology,59:8.

22. Rokeach, M. (1973). The Nature of Human Values. New York: Free Press.

23. Schwartz, S. H., and W. Bilsky. (1987). Toward A Psychological Structure of Human Values.Journal of Personality and Social Psychology, 53:12.

24. Schwartz, S. (2006). Basic Human Values: Theory, Measurement and Applications.
25. Revue Francaise de Sociologie,47 (4).

26. Hofstede, G. (2001). Culture's Consequences: Comparing Values, Behaviours, Institutions, and Organisations Across Nations. 2nd ed. Thousand Oaks: Sage

YOUR KNOWLEDGE HAS VALUE

- We will publish your bachelor's and master's thesis, essays and papers

- Your own eBook and book - sold worldwide in all relevant shops

- Earn money with each sale

Upload your text at www.GRIN.com and publish for free

.